Concert at the Arts Centre

T0342772

By Julie Haydon

Illustrations by Meredith Thomas

Contents

Students' News

My Ballet Concert

Last Sunday I took part in my ballet school's end-of-year concert.

The concert was held at the arts centre.
It was for family and friends.
It started at 2 pm and finished at 4 pm.

I performed in two dances.

In the first dance, I was a fairy,

so I had to wear a pretty pink dress with small wings.

Mum put some make-up on my face

and white flowers in my hair.

When the music started,
we ran onto the stage in a line
and began to dance.

The orchestra played beautiful music as we danced.

After the group dance, I had to do a solo dance.
Mum and Dad watched from the front row,
and Dad took some photos of me.

At first I was nervous, then I began to enjoy myself.
Everyone clapped loudly when I had finished.

The final dance was about a fierce fire in a forest
that destroyed many trees.
The dance tells how the trees grew back.
Some of us danced the part of the fire.
We wore red and yellow costumes,
and we had red and black streamers in our hair.

The end-of-year ballet concert was very special for everyone.

Our Local Arts Centre

Our local arts centre is three years old.
The brick building is very modern
and there is a large car park outside.

People enter the building by going up concrete steps and walking through a large doorway.
Inside the arts centre there is an area called a foyer.
People who come to see a show
wait in the foyer until it is time to go into the theatre.

The theatre has many rows of seats
in front of a large stage.
The seats are much higher than the stage.
There is also an orchestra pit between the stage
and the first row of seats, where the orchestra plays
during a show.

The theatre has lots of lights and speakers.
The lights are turned down
when it is time for a show to start.
Music, voices and other sounds come through the speakers.

A thick curtain covers the stage.
The curtain is opened when a show starts
and closed when the show finishes.

There are rooms behind the stage.
Some of these are dressing rooms for the performers,
and some are rooms for the costumes and props.

People in our city enjoy our new arts centre.